to my father,

you have always been the one

to teach me there is sun after storm;

this is what i've done with it.

to the reader,

this book tells the voyage of fifteen years. in your hands you

hold my days, my dusks, my darknesses, my dawns.

the path from hurting to healing. my only wish

is that you will find *something* to learn from it.

contents:

the day - 4

the dusk - 36

the dark - 62

the dawn - 94

the day;

the part that drowns in sunlight, it focuses on the points

in ones life that appear as if they could not become higher.

i may not look it but
i have fire in my eyes
and a seraphic soul
i am the pages inside this book
so narrow you will see right through
but you will never be able
to defy the words
that are pitying from my wrists
read me
they beg
why don't you

(g.k.)

some people say i am grass valleys,
summer sunsets and
moonlit lakes in the middle of march.
but the truth is that i have never been that soft.
i am a fire storm
seaside thunder
and the bellowing of mountains before they fall.
i have ravines on my skin
that have taken lives of the innocent
and oceans in my eyes that have made homes
out of bodies that were empty.
i have only ever been
the center of a hurricane
and if you are wanting someone
who keeps their voice quieter
than the surface of the moon
then that someone
you are looking for
isn't me.

(g.k.)

theories of the universe.

• only the present exists. the past and the future are a mere idea of the mind. last christmas doesn't exist, nor does my graduation day, nor does this passage as i write it. i never sliced my palm open in fifth grade, or sprained my ankle in eighth. i never was able to say to myself that i made it.

• white holes are somewhere out there. cause if black ones have the ability to diminish, or absorb entities, then an opposite object must have the ability to birth, or release them. if the universe is smart enough to create something from destruction maybe it cares enough about what has destroyed me.

• parallel universes. the vast black sea in which we live is just that; vast. maybe it's possible for it to be enveloped with alternative worlds and lifelines. cause with every decision there is an option you didn't take, maybe in some other universe you *did* take the latter. maybe in some other universe i have it better. maybe i have it worse.

• our origin was a black hole. everything a black hole digests has the possibility of creating an infinite chain of newborn universes. maybe we were formed that way, too. like a flower, we started in dark ground, but look how strong we've grown our garden.

• solipsism. maybe all of this doesn't exist. at all. only i do.
maybe this note doesn't mean anything, or this book, or the
air i breathe. what if i really am as alone as i thought i could be or
none of what i'm writing matters or if it'll even reach farther
than my fingertips.

• our universe is an ocean. some places are deep and dense,
others are warm and soft. it is not just one
incomplete-never-ending-repetitive force. there are blips and
glimpses of highs and lows. it's beautiful how the universe, too,
can have some imperfections.

(g.k.)

it will either drip down your chin
like a downpour
you weren't prepared for
or it will seize the air
in your lungs.
it could twist your knuckles
backward
or kiss the
back part
of your palm
you will taste
salt water
and soap
it may be trying to cleanse you
or leave you on the floor
but don't be afraid
it is only love
and love would never want to
hurt you

– only love

(g.k.)

i am so young
but so naive
i think i have the whole world
at my feet
i know so much
yet so little
there are feelings i have never
kissed
and people i have never felt
i am so silly to presume
there is not much left to learn
about the earth and
about myself.

— open minded

(g.k.)

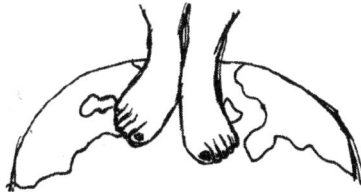

for my future child,

my arms will be your lean-to. your mountain crest. your safe haven. when something begins to mold inside your stomach i will hold you against my headboard until the lamp on my bedside table burns black. i will be the water you need and the sunlight you strive for. i will show you all beauty, and how there is more beneath your toes. years from now, when i become a mother, i will raise a child who's threaded clean. no promises, no catches, no finer print. if you come into this world afraid, i will show you why it's okay to be.

(g.k.)

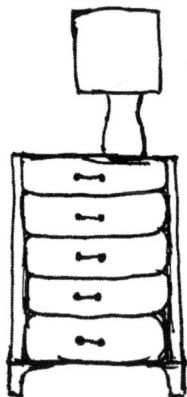

one day
i will make something of myself.
perhaps this body
wasn't just meant for breathing
perhaps i'll become something more.
something better.
something worthwhile.
cause i have to face it
the bones in my body are brittle
and the tone in my voice is stale
but the pound in my heart
thumps louder
than any sadness that will crush me.
one day
i will make something of myself.
whether that be
inventing a revolutionary
head-turning
necessity or simply
sharing my existence with the world.
perhaps i really am here for a reason
for a someone
and perhaps that someone is me

— i don't know why i'm here yet but
maybe that's how it's supposed to be

(g.k.)

once in a while, you are going to fall. this is inevitable. you could be at your strongest mountain peak but it will still disappear beneath you. and you are going to blame yourself, trust me, you are going to convince yourself that you are at fault. that you are your own weak link. the broken fraction of a whole. but let me remind you that recovery, by definition is 'a return to a normal state of health, mind, or strength.' like everything else in this world, recovery does not promise a forever. there is no label telling you that this is it- you find the end of the journey and there is nothing left to overcome. it is really anything but all that. prepare yourself for it.

we are all waiting together for the answers to our questions and for the confusion in our minds to be at peace. we are waiting for the point when every fragment becomes connected, when the road is fully paved and our eyes can finally see the way. but what we forget is that a puzzle is only made of paper. it will never be invincible. sometimes roads aren't stable and neither is the sky. and when all this happens, we mistake it for weakness; we say *i did not try hard enough* or *i'm not as strong as i thought*. we are mistaking balance for weakness and mistreating ourselves in fault of the fateful.

you've risen, you've smiled, you've fallen and cried. when it's been raining a little too hard, you wait for sunshine. when wind comes a little too strong, you wait for the calm. but don't tell me, that you've never wanted thunder.

cause in droughts you wait for water,

and in endless days you wait for gray.

so when you're hurting you wait for happiness

and when you're happy you wait for pain.

– the beginning of equilibrium

(g.k.)

14

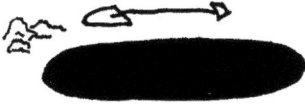

you'll burrow under soil
to avoid the immovable hills
and forests made of porcupine quills
but you'll eventually come out
the other end
so maybe this isn't a hole you
are stuck in
maybe this is a pathway
needing to be finished.
maybe the hardest way
is the quickest.

— what if

(g.k.)

things that make me happy (read when feeling sad)

- long hugs.
- flower fields.
- catching a shooting star.
- speaking up for myself.
- being kind to people and watching their face light up.
- clean bed sheets.
- goosebumps while experiencing something astonishing.
- laughing until my stomach hurts.
- sand between my toes.
- smelling something familiar and remembering where it's from.
- loving unconditionally.
- knowing that every day i receive a new beginning,

and only i can choose what to do with it.

(g.k.)

genna kinn

hope will tug at your toes
until you're reminded
that she's there for
you and
faith will unfold your
eyes when you're in
need so you feel safe
again and
love will stitch all those
scars and make you
believe that you
have been worth it
cause remember that
you have been
all along

(g.k.)

i crave a love as deep as cataracts
window panes would cry.
i want hands made of fog
and floods
and freedom
lips to translate a thousand
different tongues.
hips that sway like swerving roads,
teeth like a punishment
and eyes like an antidote.
i want riptides to devour me
deeper than an oceans cream
dressed in curtains and bows.
i yearn for breath as low as catacombs
and hope that flows through blood and bone
i want to smile so hard i drown
to live so freely i fly
to break so easily i am remade new
every
single
time.

(g.k.)

it's not when you receive
four PhD's
a job that pays plumply
or someone who gives you half of
what could have been whole.
worth comes with your existence
not in what we've been taught it's found in.
you receive purpose when
you come out
of your mothers womb not
when you live according
to what everyone else
expects you to.

— worth should have been
your middle name

(g.k.)

my purpose
is not to be beautiful
my existence
is not wrapped around the journey
to become
radiant
or wanted
i am not here to be devoured
by those who
appreciate my beauty nor
devour myself when
i believe i am.
i am here to exist
in heartbeats and exhales
and whether i become appealing
in the process
is something no one
is going to decide
for me.

(g.k.)

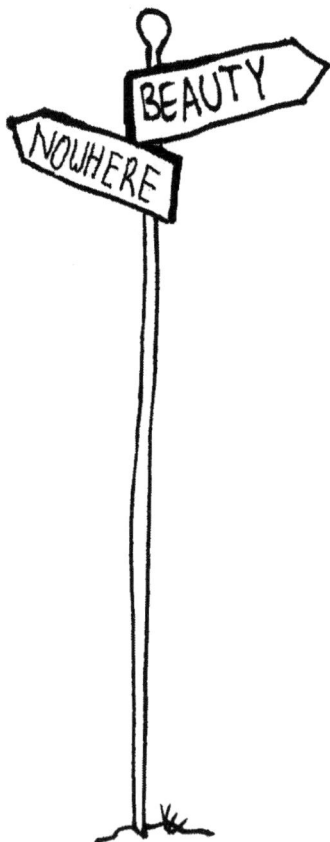

the only constant in life is the inconstant.

the changed.

the revised.

the modified.

the only thing you can promise yourself is the end. and to be safe, that should be it. i don't owe anything to this universe, to this world, besides the thank you note for granting me the ability to have strength and compassion. in fact it's given me so much more than just that. but then again, i only loosely fit the definition of thankful.

i can appreciate all sorrow; for we have treated the earth with such pain and ignorance. but the people beneath this sky expect me to sacrifice myself for the sake of being kind. i do not owe myself to this world. i do not owe myself to anyone.

actually, the only person i owe anything to is me. for the pain and ignorance i've caused myself on my own behalf is far greater than any man could ever know. the punishments i've endured to my mind and body would be considered malicious if wished on anyone else.

so no, i do not owe the *world* every bit of me,

i owe *myself* just that.

(g.k.)

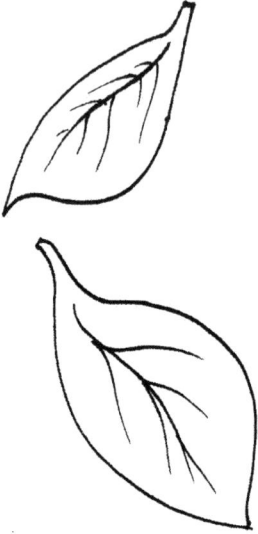

men are compared to mountains
as woman are to leaves
but i think someone got it backwards
men do not have to concave in
from snow
and be built the size of
seven stacked forests
nor do women
have to be thinly sliced
twirling downwards from
where they should be headed.
i've met boys that have
eyes twined into gardens
hands as smooth as almonds and
girls who have intuition as fierce
as a roaring sea.
we are all more than mountains.
we are all more than leaves.

– not all men are strong; not all women are weak.

(g.k.)

the air that was inside you
for less than three seconds
has touched
window panes
and mountain views
it's been inhaled by towers
and streams
and milk
and bread.
it's been reiterated underneath
cobble streets
and above wood-plank rooftops
it's been loved beneath sheets
and hands
between cold countries
and one million suns.
the air inside you has
traveled so far
to get to you,
does that not feel comforting
at all.

(g.k.)

her mind would burst every night
full of pulsing galaxies.
each memory she had contained
billions of stars and
billions of solar systems
each thought she had would hold
billions of planets and
billions of life forms
she was the thing that held
all worlds together.
her body was enigmatic;
unfathomable.
her hips waved more than
the ocean's goodbyes
and her tongue caressed deeper than
a storms confusion.
her touch was softer than stardust
but hit you harder than lightening.
she held hands with thunder,
lived in the eye of a tornado and
still managed to give you the universe.
she is unearthly,
and you treated her like a girl.

— but she is so much more

(g.k.)

maybe you don't have their eyes

        or their hair

        or their voice

        or their skin

    or the bounce in their belly

    when they laugh

        or their gaze that shakes

        the speech out of throats

    but you have

    all of you

    and that might be even better.

— how to (not) compare

(g.k.)

coalesce

i want to taste the sugar
between the stars' silk palms
but i will have to wait until i find
the human equivalent.

– i wonder when they'll come.

(g.k.)

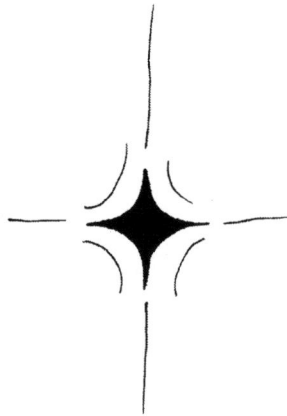

the universe seems to take time on some things.
the thread between my drywall.
and the cracks inside my palms.
the speckled skin
on my brothers chin
the way the wind blows
without
needing
any
effort
at
all.
the sky was well rested
when it made its cloudy bed
as was the sea when it settled
on top of the shore.
the universe was so calm that day
it could have made thunder
from only
it's smile.
it took a breather
while carving yours and
a break before painting those eyes.
i guess it couldn't quite fathom
how exquisite you were
and i guess
neither could i.

— when they aren't just human

(g.k.)

if we love like beauty
it will fall
before we even get a chance to catch it.
like moonlight
serene
and smooth
our velvet tongues
will tie knots in our stomachs.
this is not how we are supposed to be.
you love me like city lamps
broken and boring
nobody wants to fix it
just flicker when
the timing is right.
i don't want to be loved
prettily or mellowed
love me like a
wilted rose
like bloody oceans and
fingernails between my gums
i want to be loved so hard
i have to look at the world twice
cause it's so unfamiliar to me.

(g.k.)

remain a melodic anomaly
your skin as smooth
as a harpists hands
you don't have to be brutal
to be heard
it's okay to be stripped
to the bone
as long as you believe
you can still move mountains
sometimes the softest thunder
will burn your stomach harder
be the calm
that people trust
so easily.

— less

(g.k.)

it has to be the stars
and how they cease inside the sea
but purr before entering.
or the out-casted lights from kitchens
that melt into the street
the ominous way the sky
folds over
and over
itself
not wanting to come to any barrier
to stay where water is just below
lukewarm.
there is a forest fire charring
the lining of my stomach
reminding me
that while nothing matters
everything
also matters
that if i want to breathe i must breathe
if i want to love i must love
and if i want to live
it will never be that hard
to just exist
contently.

(g.k.)

she is the cosmos in a dress made of stars. she dances to the sound of moon rays, planets that weep story endings and she guides you with the whispering wind. she smiles as peaceful as feathers and fate. it's freedom to be able to dream underneath her atmosphere.

she is the smoke from the hearth and tastes like charcoal and chamomile tea, she's an herb garden of sage and rosemary. she'll hold you in patches like the sun does the earth but she'll let you breathe in ease. her hair is brushed like briar patches. leaves fall from her lips. she's the breezeway between mountains and streams.

she is a water monster, making love to the waves. she communicates in whirlpools and sea tornadoes and hurricanes and storms. she will blaze you to the depths if you anger her, but she'll let you pass if you don't. her voice is that of a siren, alluring cause it lures you into the depths of her land, she loves you, she'll save you, if you let her.

she is the sound of music. the sound of choruses and ballads. tunes twist away from her tooth gap and there's no saying who she will seduce next. she's a piano of keys, different doors same destination. smile like songs of harps and moonlight, vines against cellos and thorns against flutes. she's ancient love songs and reborn poetry.

— a tribute to women

(g.k.)

31

the first time he calls you
beautiful
you are naked.
leave the man.
he should have uttered
perfection
when you smiled

— you are the most elegant thing
i have ever seen

(g.k)

my problem was
i thought my whole
existence was inscribed in stone
she isn't a princess until
her prince comes and rescues her
so i'd walk haphazardly
like a body
without brains
just half a beating heart
waiting for the rest of it.
but when i figured out that
i could love myself before
anyone else was allowed to
i took that stupid slate and said
maybe i'm not a princess
maybe i'm already
a queen

— god, was it worth it

(g.k.)

you were oak trunks
>and wheat leaves
>>you were grown beneath soil

and high above clouds.
>you finished forest lines
>>and filled empty space

you made the world feel needed.
you became fragile streams and sandy bays
>you were the seashore seagulls

and garden jays.
>before walking this planet
>>you were once apart of it.

— you are still just as beautiful

(g.k.)

the only reason they say money buys them happiness is
cause they let the things that can be bought
determine how happy they are.

— the most expensive things will never be worth
any currency

(g.k.)

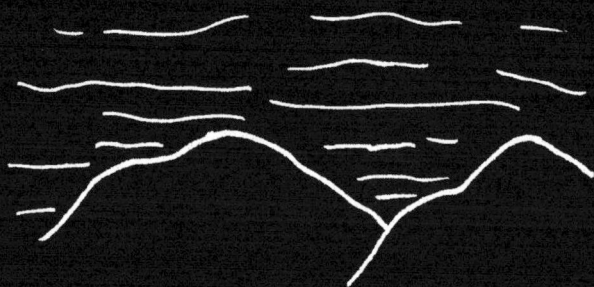

the dusk;

the part in which shadows grow, musk begins to linger and pain
tries to break our bones.

a paper cut hurts cause paper isn't smooth.
there are microscopic points on the edge, like a wood saw.
it is cutting right through you.

and the ones that leave hurt because they promised not to.
they are similar to a thunder storm cause their path ends up going
right
through
you.

— falsified forecast.

(g.k)

you won't look in the mirror
unless the lights are off.
but still
your eyes are closed.

— insecurity

(g.k.)

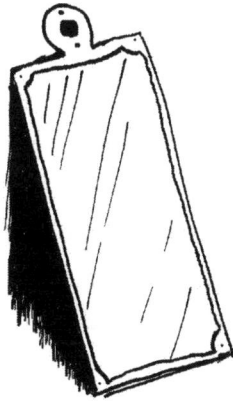

nothing is forever
so i said
i am sorry.
    but i have asked the moon
    so many more times
    then i have blinked in my
    entire life:
why am i alone?
    she cried into the ocean
    and told me
    it's cause i chose to be.

(g.k.)

the side of the highway
the smell of her sweater
the occasional crash of headlights on the open sea
i felt her hands and
they were soft
they were melodious
creating tunes between our fingertips and rhythm
beneath our palms. i unfelt my feelings
what was scratching at my ankles
and with fear under my finger nails
and bravery bunched in my bones
i stood up
in silence.
i tightened my knuckles
and without a deep breath
i left the side of the highway
the smell of her sweater
and the crash of headlights into the sea
cause i knew i wasn't ready for the possible conclusion
of her not wanting me
i knew that i'd need to wait till the day
that wanting myself would be more
than i could ever
possibly ask for

— i am young and i don't yet want to be in love

(g.k)

lust takes us for granted
down beneath the sea.
while envy sings
from the tops of trees.
anger will foam on the rim
of a champagne glass
as resentment blushes in bed.
sometimes the most horrid things can
be found in such beautiful places
maybe it's only coincidence that
this earth is considered art.

— when the salt *tastes* like sugar

(g.k.)

she's a bleeding lump of
unneeded epiphanies.
the sky is milk and she vomits
her veins into the clouds
you plead her to stop
but she won't cause
you don't ever try to save
someone who doesn't think
they need to be.

(g.k.)

it's almost as if we base our
entire existence around
the way we look
in someone else's eyes
rather than the way
we really are
in our very own.

(g.k.)

when star systems stop colliding
and realize their intimacy has gotten
the better of them
you'll see them breathe slowly
heavily
they will hesitantly sink above the sky
rubbed clean with water and remade.
if they remember how to
their air will exasperate your tongue
you will inhale their blood and sweat,
their bones.
you are the second hand creation of all
that ever was
if one day it shall perish,
than you shall perish too.

— a sad sort of promise

(g.k.)

it was a balmy summer afternoon
when the waves whistled a story
i asked for the ending but
they wouldn't yet say.
it was a tale of the sea
and how long ago
it fell so deeply
in love with the sun
that it would do anything
just to touch the surface
so it tried to fly and it tried to swim
and it tried to climb to kiss her
but it was never quite far enough.
i asked if he ever got the chance to hold her.
it retreated so i could
see her still shining
in the sky.

— sometimes it just isn't meant to be

(g.k.)

i try so hard to be balanced.
to become an aura of black and white
and the backbone of the sea
i see people walk the streets
dressed in satin and leather
and others
with overalls and jeans
i keep trying
to be the center piece.
but the reality is
some days i am breath being held
for seventy-two seconds
and the city lights that get
mistaken for stars.
while other times i am
the bruised dough
of a thumb
and blood beneath the bathtub.
i just can't remember
the last time
i found myself
in the middle.

(g.k.)

human skin is made
of newspaper and glue
of stories no one bothers to read.
but there are some people
who were born between seconds
and find poetry in each paragraph
pasted behind our ankle bones.
unfortunately those same people
are the ones that can't quite
put two and two together.
those same people are the ones
who die fighting.
who see beauty in the world
cause they were made from it.

— why the world needs people like you

(g.k.)

genna kinn

and the sky will crack open
ask why i am crying behind
a closed door
i will bend my rib bones outward
and show him i am rotting from
my head to my toes
with an awry smile
he will do the same
and i will realize we have both
been broken.

— where is the storm that's named after me

(g.k.)

she sat at the toes of peasants
and sobbed into the soil
swore she's deserving only
of what she's been given
so she never tried to find anything else.
truth is no one comes
to save you
you must have the courage
and the strength
to save yourself.

— the princess or the poor

(g.k.)

i am growing up without the figure
that was supposed to teach me
who i am meant to be.
which means i drift
separately
and steadily.
i knew what it was like to be left
before i understood the letters in
abandonment.
i'm trying to say that
i don't have much to give
but i can promise you
i will love you with everything
i have left in me.

— i am the daughter without a mother

(g.k.)

clean your room
and do your chores
and get straight A's
is what they keep saying.
so you must do everything
they tell you to. it's the *guidance*
it's the *looking after you* but
what they do not know is that
the children that turn to robots
cause their parents wired them so
will move out after high school
and have no where left to go.
no its not the
guidance
it's the
not letting them live on their own.

— what happens to the kids who grow under pressure

(g.k.)

i am so bored of repetitive patterns
sometimes i think i'd rather spend
my whole life falling
then on stable ground.

(g.k.)

i have backspaced this poem
at least nine times
cause i am so afraid of saying
the wrong things
of speaking in the way
i didn't want to
or didn't intend to
this just shows how
such simple things
fill me with such
heavy anxiety.
i'll make my bed-
or attempt to
at least nine times
cause it doesn't quite look right
i am so overwhelmed by such
irrelevant things
i'm beginning to think
there's something wrong with me.
i could spend an entire day
in the corner of my room
biting the nails
of the mistakes
i am replaying in my mind
at least nine times
each.
i wonder if i will ever
be able to speak to the sky
without the fear it will
fall asleep.

(g.k.)

what is average if no two people are the same
what is normal if someone can
recite Shakespeare from memory
but another can sense danger
quicker than anybody else can.
what is run-of-the-mill
if he has the voice of a thunder storm
but she has the skill of Tchaikovsky
if someone is fluent in seven languages
but somebody else can twist their tongue
seven different ways
this world is so peculiar trying
to fit everyone inside a corridor
and make them look
the exact same
you will never be like them
that is supposed to be
a good thing.

(g.k.)

legend says there was land
where lovers could roam
without fear
of being forsaken.
they kissed goodnight
below the black moon
cause they knew there would be
tomorrow.
i have dreams
of my hair
gleaming in these fields
in these valleys
you'd get lost in
i can't just explain the feeling
in my belly when
i wasn't scared anymore.
i knew
if i brought love
into that world
it would always be
brought back to me

(g.k.)

i am weather;
in the sense that
i can range from
calm cumulus clouds
to a downpour of rain, proud
of the sound i make
on the ground,
but i am not weather;
in the sense that
i feel and breathe
and cry underneath.
there are two versions of me
the one that i am
and the one that you see.

(g.k)

as gravity gets lighter
bark strips not towards earth but sky.
while sand and sea are bubbling upward
we are stuck on the cement cause of how hard we relied.
only nature knows that sometimes putting faith
into stable things that have
a possibility of changing
are deadlier than
the change
itself.

(g.k.)

i have decided that
from this day on
my heart will no longer
beat for someone else
it will beat for
me
the body it was built for
the body it was put in
to pump blood
between oxygen.
cause before i was clever enough
to realize people take advantage,
my heart would beat for others.
the ones i thought it was built for
the ones i gave it to
in hopes i'd get
theirs back
in return

— i never did

(g.k.)

we are not
angels who want to go home
or tiny teenage girls
who need boys to
sweep us off our feet
we are not
tragically beautiful
we are
humans in pain
and
beauty has nothing
to do with it.

— stereotypical sadness

(g.k)

the sun is in love
so the moon can travel north
and fields can revive soil and salt
orchids don't grow coal
they bud sapphire fruit
we know what rain smells like
and so does the sky cause
the sun is in love
with the planets
and the planets are in love with the sun
when you are in love it should blossom
there should never
be any harm done.

(g.k)

my whole life people
would project their expectations
of themselves
onto my impressionable forehead
so i'd cry
cause i didn't know
what they said i did.
now at fifteen, i still feel
obliged to know my fix.
if i knew how to save myself
would it not make sense
i would have done so already.

– common knowledge that isn't so common

(g.k.)

its a bit upsetting knowing that
we all have the capability to bring deep
affection
into the lives of those who
keep us warm
but we also have the choice of flaming
others with our tongue
and wrecking the esteem
some worked so hard
to find
if we'd like
we can spend days screeching at them
to watch blood drip from their ear drums
its not that difficult
to love and i have yet
to truly grasp
why some people still choose
to damage.

(g.k.)

he tells me i am too hard to swallow
that i am more blade
than i am bone
that i suck the veins out of fingers
and the knuckles out of thumbs
i am too difficult to be handled
he forgets
i have handled myself
my whole life
i know how draining it is
to try and take care of me
and that sometimes
i want to give up trying,
too

– what part of exhausting
didn't you get

(g.k)

as long as your child is safe
why does it matter
what
makes them happy.
if he wants to kiss boys
or if she was born one
all you have to do
is love them
as hard as you did before.

– to the parents

(g.k.)

they say pain is so demanding
but really so is
love
you know how tough it is
to break habits.
being sad is
what you want to know.
so it isn't surprising
you haven't yet figured out
how to be fond
of things
with better intentions.
how to get attached
without missing home.

− 28 days to break this

(g.k.)

they must know that artists
best create while hurting
so it's understandable
that my bad days
lead to better art

– this is how i get it out

(g.k.)

the dark;

the part where we can't fall asleep unless our eyes are open,

we are bleeding from the outside in.

coalesce

we are living in a world
where hearing each other
is the same thing
as listening
but when i scream at you
in the height of my lungs
LISTEN TO ME
you tell me
lower your voice
i can hear you.
i don't want to be heard
i want to be listened to
i want to be remembered.

— please pay attention

(g.k.)

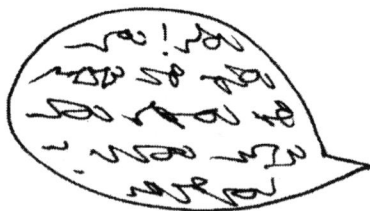

70

the one thing that will never fail to leave my stomach shaking is when i hear the confession

'i love you,

more than anything'.

cause that shouldn't be the case. humans can be beautiful but they could never create bands of alabaster and beige like the sun does to the sky. they could never make us feel the way singing does or bubble baths or bay windows or clouds that are shaped like fireworks or being able to smile at the world underneath. the closest another human shall ever get to us is when our fingertips are laced together in love. and while that may be enough for some, nobody will ever be as close to us as we are with ourselves.

when you begin to confess

'i love you, more than anything'.

you are really saying

'i love you, more than myself'

and no one

i repeat

no one

should ever get that opportunity.

(g.k.)

it hurts my heart
when i see
that some people look at colours
and believe some
are more worthy than others.
to those i speak about above:
if you presume that someone
is valued less than you
just for the shade in which
their organs are wrapped
i must break the news;
we all have blood
bones
and a beating heart
but then again with
that kind of statement
you, my friend
might not.

(g.k.)

genna kinn

they wake up after the sun dies
and feel safer in the dark
watch them kick tomorrow
under the carpet cause
they don't want to see it anymore.
they start to drive with their eyes
off the road and
their hands against the windows.
remember all they need
is a word with four
letters
and a syllable that sticks
to your tongue.
a wrist to pull them out
of oblivion.
all they need is the feeling of
this is what it's like to be okay.
so give them that
just tell them

— stay

(g.k.)

when i remember her fingers
against my cheek
or her words
against my eardrums
i get angry.
she thought i
was the root
of all evil
at only age two.
when she calls
my brother on the phone
and tells him she misses him
i feel our wood flooring creak
i want to ask why she doesn't
miss me
i want to tell her i know
what it's like to ache
i came from the same pain
you grew from
it feels bittersweet
i want her
but i don't
and i know she's not at fault
cause she couldn't help
being born
a little different
than the rest of us
but i am still afraid of getting
a little too
close.

— malfunctioned

(g.k.)

be blunt rather than subtle
thorough rather than vague
you'll discover who's
there to love you
and who's around to
try and get their way.

— be safe not sorry

(g.k.)

no they did not bruise you
but they broke you and that
is still
abuse.

— no blood but still there is pain

(g.k.)

if death looks at you through your window
you must shove him off as if it's really
nothing new.
if he smiles at you with bullet-shell teeth,
and breath that smells like
the air beneath a gravestone
then smile back
unwounded.
and if you wake up at two in the afternoon
while he's in the corner of your room
look him in the eyes
while your chest bleeds into your collarbones
and tell him to come back soon.
he will.
he will sit and whisper things
along the lines of
trepidation.
he will ask if you are afraid.
the ground will crumble.
ask him if there is a reason
you should be.

— is there

(g.k)

she screams in idiom
you haven't yet heard of
cause her mother did the same
as her mother and
hers before that.

if you can open the truth
behind broken hearts
and how they are passed down
from father to daughter
from mother to son,
then your own child
won't have to bear
the noise between your teeth.

cause somewhere in your throat
your pain comes out as anger.
when you try to cry
you scream in idiom
your child hasn't yet
heard of
(make sure they don't ever have to)

— broken parents raise broken kids

(g.k.)

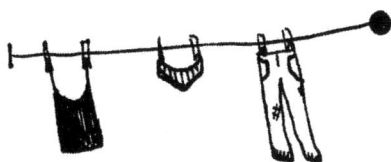

i must meet the status quota.
mention the word
love
at least eight times
before the end of
this poem.
cause that's what they want
to be reminded that sometimes
love doesn't work out
love doesn't fix things the way
everyone says it should have.
they want to read passages about how
you would undress me out of love
but told me to take the bus home
or how you rung out my skin against
the drying rack and
i still came back
they want to hear me say
i will always come back
cause it's comforting to know
that someone else can hear
their heart depleting
it's comforting to know
that you're not the only one
who's crying cause
you can't yet fix it.

— four short

(g.k.)

all these quotes
these passages
these poems
are about you
you're an unscripted name
an unspoken word.
you are pronouns
and emotions
without a human to feel them.
all the things i
write,
i write for you.
so i'm sorry
that i don't write about love,
it's just that
you never really gave it to me.

— crotchet

(g.k.)

when they tell you they've changed
i don't want you to listen.
i want you to watch.
i want you to watch their fingers try
to find their way above your backbone
and how they distract you
with a flick of their tongue.
i want you to notice how they smile
as if someone's watching
blink as if they've never learnt how.
i want you to remember the pattern
of their footsteps
after they're finished
and how far they bow their head
towards the floor.
when someone tells you
that they've changed.
you don't listen.
you learn.
you learn that they
most likely
haven't.

— the case for most, unfortunately.

(g.k.)

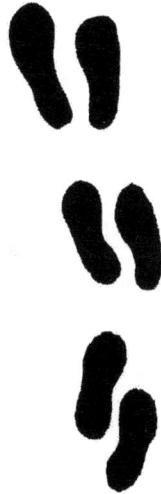

the only thing i have ever known
to a depth greater than the sea
is how to be afraid
of something
i am not sure has ever even existed.
the only indication i get
of its presence
is the rotting of my lungs
the contraction to the point
i cannot breathe.
it's not the crowds
it's not the unknown
it's not the temperament i
was born with
or the static in the air
i seem to be in-immune from.
if i knew what it was called
i'd tell you
but i don't
and ironically
that itself
scares me.

— anxiety

(g.k.)

i have hair like my mother's
my eyes, my body
come from her too
my stubbornness
my smile
the way i can make it seem
like i really do
know what i'm speaking of.
i don't look like my fathers daughter
and it's a little cynical
cause i've always felt safer with him
than i ever have with her.

— being her child shouldn't scare me but here we are.

(g.k.)

i was a damsel in a tower
stuck falling asleep
to dragons wings
and uprising screams
i will forever be hesitant of
sounds that break the barrier of calm
cause they sound so much
like my mother.

— (ir)rational fear

(g.k)

the thunder king beats his drum
and all castles crumble. he is taking back
what has been stolen from.
humans are all this earth has-
we are all it could ever need
but someone changed the story
so that we continue to kill
our origin and
each other in the process.
we have had wars made of guns cause
some people would rather watch
death than prevent it.
one day the thunder king
will beat his drum
and our scrapers will crumble.
he will take back
what we have stolen cause
we never knew how lucky we were
to call this place
a home.

— prophetic catastrophe

(g.k.)

there are two sides to a line
the left
and the right
the fight or the flight
you have to play
devils advocate to get the answer.
and i do wish things were simpler
less words
more quiet
less soft
more firm
but there are two sides to a line
and two faces to a coin
there are opposite ends of the earth
and double strings of DNA
the answer is never simple
it is never just
one.
you are neither tapeworms
nor sheep
awake
nor asleep
but you are either alive
or you're not here
at all.

— if it was simple i'd spell it out for you but remember
this is a poem

(g.k.)

sometimes the hardest thing
about my day
is when i have so much to bleed
but no opening
for it to come through.

— if i am silent.

(g.k.)

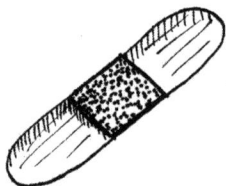

band-aids above nonexistent bruises
to the way you don't have enough for real ones now.
we would laugh while
little hands would fix things
that never needed fixing.
i had fingers made of
flesh and bone and dreams
has there ever been such things
as story book endings.
blanket stitching of moon beams
and magic beans
i only have enough for one white sheet
this has never been the same
as what i thought it'd be.

— don't spend your youth growing up.

(g.k.)

inconvenience is when you
must write something happy
but you haven't even smiled
in the past four days.
it's like a puzzle.
to write happy
i must be happy
but to be happy
i must write it.

— i don't know if this counts or not

(g.k.)

the secret is that
nobody has everything
figured out
nobody knows
exactly what to do
or where to go
or who to love
some are just so very good
at acting like it

(g.k.)

he spoke his passions and his fears and the secrets he kept buried
under land mines. but he spoke them to the stars cause those were
the only ones who'd listen.

— you didn't and look where he's ended up

(g.k.)

connect all living lines and you will realize
you use who uses you
that is what the equation
starts with.
it is not a selfless act of putting
others before our own
it is nothing but the egocentric
way that humans are.
it's a shame that we do things this way
always a little for ourselves
and maybe sometimes
for the greater good
for the happiness of humanity.
but even when we lose someone
we cry not because they have left
but cause they have left *us*.
cause they are no longer here
to give us what they had been.

(g.k.)

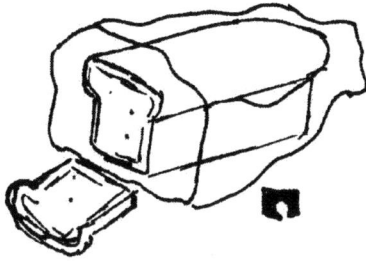

why do we try so hard to
eat simplicity like it's the first
meal we've had in eight days.
i want to make messes
and create chaos i want
to forget the feeling
that the only thing in mayhem
was my mind.

(g.k.)

sometimes even the boys
with pretty pink smiles
have insides made
of greed.
for who's sake
does the hero chase a dream
besides his own

(g.k.)

genna kinn

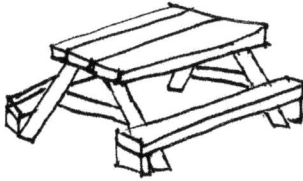

in seventh grade i was with my friends
in the lunch room when a boy i was sitting beside
put his hand on my thigh.
my blood simmered through my cheeks
but i laughed along with the rest of them.
later, my friend said
i think he likes you.
i wanted to vomit and bawl
that is not what you do
when you like someone.

— i am afraid cause nobody seems to know the fine line between
flirting and being forceful

(g.k.)

sometimes i wonder
if the sun will ever get to sleep in
roll over in his bed
and have the covers up to his cheekbones
i wonder if he will forget about
dry droughts and
dragons that extrude heat waves
bonfires and
throbbing migraines.
sometimes i wonder
if there are days i sleep in
just to forget
about the fact i am
sometimes
afraid of waking up again.

(g.k.)

they'll fold their smile around your waist to ~~find out how naive you can be~~ show you how extravagant they think you are. they'll wrap their arms around the world to prove ~~you're weak enough to be carried~~ they're strong enough to carry you. they'll kiss your cheek out of ~~selfishness~~ love. ~~cause they love you.~~

no they don't.

— if there are lines to read between, put down the book.

(g.k.)

we are cows salivating at dinner bells
and dogs begging for bones
our minds are so skilled
at association
we could cry at the sight of rainbows
and laugh at someones dread
without ever realizing
the reasoning for it.

— don't forget how powerful your head is.

(g.k.)

the day dreams in me
it wraps its wrists around my throat
and asks me why i am scared.
i say: in a world like this heaven only
exists if you pretend it does.

alright. that's fair.

— who came up with such a concept like heaven

(g.k.)

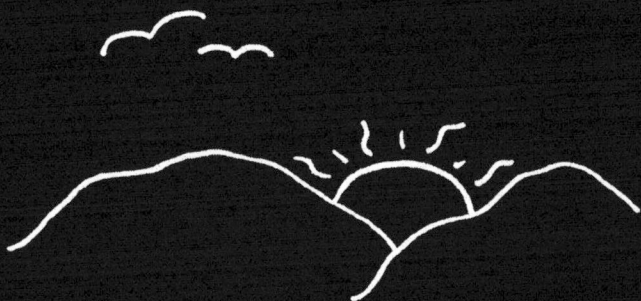

the dawn;
the part who provides healing and the taste of new beginnings;
we will find our way home.

if you grow into a flower
you will become so beautiful
girls will want to keep you
and boys will want to take you home
so flourish into a tree
with roots the size of skyscrapers
and branches that begin to fly
to touch the air
the earth
and the spirit of everything
that's ever doubted you
so you can show them
why they shouldn't have
why they shouldn't have ever said
you will never reach
the damn sky

(g.k.)

there are people out there
who won't tremble at the
absence of your bones
the breakage of your heart
and the bloodless skin
that embodies you
they will rise tall and heavy
cause they
see themselves in you.
so both stand hand in hand
and teach each other
how to breathe again.

— reflection

(g.k.)

one of my favourite things
about writing
is knowing that
there are oceans
others could not get across
but with my words
their heart
found the way.

— thank you

(g.k.)

i am not clean.
when i was a baby i'd love
to dip my toes into the rough sand
of seashores
i'd get grains underneath my
fingernails
and somehow between my teeth.
i am not clean.
i make a mess of things
i was younger and couldn't bake
without getting flour
up my nose.
i am not clean.
i am fifteen years old and
a name with nine letters
but my skin has seen so many more
brush strokes than that.
i am more than just empty
i am a mountain slope carved in
ten thousand swift winters
and a dollar that's been down
the drain.
i am a rusted ladder.
and i am used.
but i'm not ashamed
an old home will always
have more stories up its sleeve
than a new one.

— for the ones that have a history

(g.k)

he was the one to balance on tightropes
swaying above three hundred foot foam waves
just to see what was on the other side.
he'd climb mountain peaks
and jump split caverns
cause of rumours he heard about uncharted plains.
he'd tell stories of people he met and things he'd seen
but you had to listen closely
cause he'd never tell them twice.
he was never disappointed
cause he expected nothing more from life
than change.
he kissed the sky good morning
and tucked it in goodnight.
and that's why the earth
was so grateful for him.
he bled nothing but curiosity
and breathed nothing but desire.
but i guess he sought more
than this world could offer.
cause one day
he disappeared.
i don't know where he went.
but i like to think it's serving him better
than this precarious planet.
and sometimes, when the world is out quiet
and the lights are out dead
you can almost hear him telling stories with the wind
and making music with the stars.
i don't know where he went
but i will always remember what he told me.
his mantra;
the reason he was still there was cause
not everybody ran from fear
he went and chased it it

– the boy who flew away

(g.k.)

if he weeps he is not worthy
but he weeps cause he's a man
and if showing emotion
and sensation overload
is supposed to determine your value
whats the excuse for infants
that are born crying

(g.k)

your life can begin again
whenever you'd like it to
tomorrow
today
right now
you are never limited
to possibilities
you can take control.
despite everyone telling you
that you're out of it.

(g.k.)

in this land of the lost and forgotten
we plead to be a priority
that exceeds all else.
we type contracts signing off
our limbs and organs
to people we've only just met
in the slightest chance
they will have more use for it
than we ever did
cause in the end,
we are so accustomed to
bluffers that
being used doesn't seem
so painful anymore but
i think that's where we're wrong.
cause we all stand together
with missing hearts and bloody palms,
and maybe this time
we can agree
that we are all worth more
than we acted out to be
and that no matter how many faults
we expand to,
only one of those faults
will be rightly convicted.
and that is our fault
for making ourselves believe
that we were ever
anything less
than worthy.

— seven billion hearts on seven billion sleeves

(g.k.)

remember that behind greed
and fear and ego and reputation
there is raw human.
unfelt.
untouched.
unsteady.

— take that how you will

(g.k.)

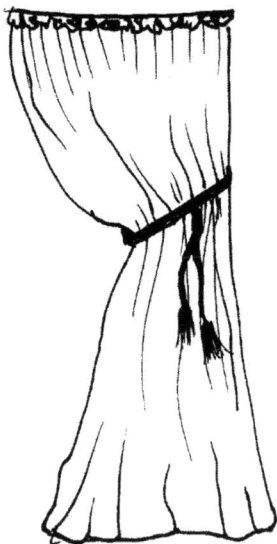

you told me i was the moon
and while i thought that meant
i lit up a dark sky,
you meant it as
i am the reflection
of those who shine,
that i'm only here when the sun
is gleaming bright enough.
but i am not the moon
and you are not the sun.
in fact i am my own supernova
and i will shine with my own explosions
and i will burn until i implode
and i will be my own light within eternity.
you are you and i am i.
and that is the very end of it.

— i am not a missing piece i will always be whole.

(g.k.)

the east will love the west
it will kiss her in the sky
and show the cosmos in between
the gaps of their fingers.
if you pay attention
the immortal stars will
march forward
wherever forward
ends up to be.
if you pay attention
your stomach will yearn
cause the iron
in your blood
matches the cosmos
and it wants to find its
way home.
it will grumble and beat
and thump like the hum
of the ocean tide
and if you are lucky enough
you will find someone who
makes you feel the way
this earth does.

— soulmate; /ˈsōlˌmāt/; noun; the human form of inhuman love.

(g.k.)

rocks and clay
must certainly be the same.
the ability to be mounded and changed
and created into something
that can only be imagined.
one takes centuries
the other minutes
but despite how long
they can both be brought
from minerals
to delicacy.

— i promise you'll get there

(g.k.)

i am afraid of the dark.
i am afraid of bugs
and clowns-
the usual.
the way the plane vibrates
before it leaves ground
it feels like it's pouring the air pressure
out of the cabin.
speeding on yellow, even
if it has *just* turned from green
cause how long
does it really stay that way
until red
and how long does it really take
'till you get hit.
whether the sea is calm
or strong
if it is boundless i am scared of it cause
there are so many conclusions
as to what is at the bottom
and how long it'll take to get there.
but the one thing
i will never be afraid of
is loving.
if you love the world,
it will love you back
in some way
or another.

(g.k.)

you are fifteen
why do you still believe
you must match the weight you were
at ten
or the height you were
at eleven.
you do not have to be small
to be pretty
in fact nothing above skin
makes somebody beautiful.
if you want to be pretty,
be kind
be passionate
be dependable
and most of all
drop the idea that
you're not beautiful already.

— repeat this till you believe it.

(g.k.)

we will never die beside
anything but our own arms
but then again
if living seems like
a trail you weren't ready for
or a lake too deep
and just thinking
of looking forward stirs a hurricane
in your core
i will be here to remind you,
that even if you
end up with only yourself
you don't always have to be
that alone.

— how do i make this sound less contradictory

(g.k.)

as a little girl
a ballerina is what i had
always wanted to become.
to dance as distinctive
as oatmeal
to spin as smooth as milk
    i wanted to have the people
    who saw me
    taste cocoa and not iron
    in their stomach not their tongue.
    i wanted to show people that
    beauty
    and purity
    and happiness
    is found in everything you
    never bother looking in.
        now
        at fifteen
        i am not a ballerina
        but i somehow received the privilege
        to teach those things
        within the sentences
        i speak from my fingers
        and the words i write with
        my throat.
                and i cannot tell you
                how fulfilling it is
                to realize i have come this far
                on my very own.

      — i am sure this is my prophecy

(g.k.)

what if this existence was only
to belong to me?
it's possible one day
i will choose to share it with another
but i don't have to.
we are all taught to find love
in someone else's palms
(fairy-tales and stories tell us so)
but i can't help to be a little selfish
cause somehow i was given
the ability to love.
so forgive me
if right now i'd like
to be my own.

— i want to want myself

(g.k.)

often times our world will crumble.
tell me the last time yours did
cause if you can remember how your tongue sank
into your stomach and the ground plowed into the sea
then i am sure you can remember
the moan of thunder and the split of sky
i am sure you can remember the dark
bleeding from each
crack in the clouds
and the empty echoes that followed.
i know you remember the ache of having
nothing left
to hold on to
nothing left
to show you it will be okay.
but i have to tell you,
you're missing a very important piece.
when there is
nothing left
you seem to forget the light inside your chest
the pulse of sun and the throb of moon
you forget that this is all inside of you.
when thunder rolls and echoes cry
please remember
you have earth in between your organs
and oceans who sing under your skin
if there is
nothing left
to hold on to
it only means you have forgotten to hold on
to the one important piece.
tell me the last time you held on
to only you.

— belt buckle.

(g.k.)

and i swear the day you can smile down to the devil
will be the day you rule the world

— to fight the devil you wait till he's done

(g.k.)

my fingers and toes will one day be petals
my bones will bow inside stems
i will grow beneath indifference
and understand that broken
does not mean bad
i will never stop trying
to become correspondent in
what the head says
and what the heart wants to have

(g.k.)

i learnt from someone awhile back that, unlike man-made forest fires, natural ones are usually healthy for the trees. after a while (just like the skies and the seas) they need a fresh start. so they will scream to the heavens 'we must burn to be remade new, our bark is drying, and we are dying there must be something you can do' so lightening falls right after thunder, and tumbles from east to west. it strips forests of their misery, only for them to grow back in softer soil and moister mulch.

my point is perhaps i am the trees. maybe i need to dissolve from remnants of a believer to become something better. i am the trees cause if they can be brave and sink down into their graves, only to then come out as stronger, i think it only makes sense that this is not where i diminish, this is where i'm born into a survivor.

(g.k.)

• write until your fingers bleed
• love until you loath
• laugh until your stomach burns
• learn until you know
• cry until you're proud again
• shout till you can't breathe
• tell the truth do not pretend;
you're hurting. so let it be.

— to recovery

(g.k.)

i froth at the mouth when they tell me
they are done
finding fondness in the world
i want to wrap my fingers around their shoulders
and sigh
it is a broken heart that is hurting you
it is not love.

— don't be afraid of the things you are made of

(g.k.)

people say your pupils will pulse
when you look at someone you love.
whether this be true or not
i hope to see the day
when i look into the mirror
to find huge hazel eyes
looking right
back at me.

(g.k.)

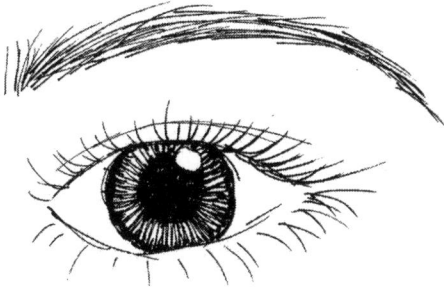

there was a woman in the bookstore
who had the most delicious eyes
her freckles were shattered on her cheeks
like shavings of coffee.
there was a lily outside of the farmers market
that looked like a hybrid of a rose
it shone like emeralds and smelled
like the sea.
i saw a mountain behind
the highway
while it wasn't the most clairvoyant thing
it did leave my spine crying.
i have fallen in love with so many things
it mustn't be that hard
for someone to do so
with me

(g.k.)

his hands are on your body
but it's still yours
his eyes are on your body
but it's still yours
he screams until you listen
you are mine
you shed and bleed
no i am my own.

— bravery

(g.k.)

17 things to save you

i. a train runs on the tracks it's been given. choose your tracks wisely.

ii. the only thing you should ever try to be is yourself. the world needs a little more of that.

iii. the man without legs wants them, but the man who has them wants more. when's the last time you were grateful for all you have been given?

iv. do not expect the world to bow at your feet after one good deed.

v. our hands can give warmth, pleasure, show anger, empathy, inflict pain, and eventually can break. you only have so much time to use them for the important things.

vi. don't pick at someone else's scabs, they already do themselves.

vii. if your cup is still half full, don't ask for more. not only will it overwhelm you, but there is one out there that is empty already.

viii. for every action there is a reaction. you pay for what you came here for.

ix. it's not fair to constantly be against yourself. you are tired because you've taught yourself to walk up stream.

x. if you want to find evil, look for fear.

xi. you are made of half pandemonium and half peace. it is up to you what to do with each.

xii. there will always be someone who insists to you that water is orange and the sky is green.

xiii. a full force gale won't move a boulder but a breeze will shuffle leaves. only you choose what you are affected by.

xiv. somebody out there has it worse. but this is you and your pain. nothing invalidates that.

xv. to someone perfection is a blank canvas, to another it's broken glass.

xvi. the way you see the world is really how you see yourself.

xvii. time will only heal wounds if they have finished hurting.

(g.k.)

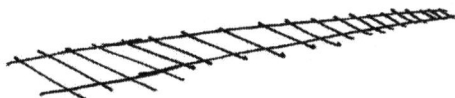

the rain knows something we don't
so it falls while we wash the dirt
off our knees
to teach us we may sometimes
hit the ground
and bleed into the pavement
but that only means we are ready
to rise back up again.

— the way it works

(g.k.)

you are my home sweet home
i'm your welcome back rug
the roof is crooked
and the nails on the walls
are falling off
but we are still in love
after all we
are still becoming.

(g.k.)

only the jeweler will know
the value of the jewel
so don't clutch my heart
and tell me i am made
of coal.

— have you forgotten where diamond comes from

(g.k)

if you ask me why i write
i will either answer with a
long winded verse
citing
Shakespeare
and Mr Allan Poe
or i'll shrug it off
and say
i just like to.
i have to admit there will
never be an answer
that sits well enough
in either of our stomachs
so we will both just have to accept that
maybe
we will never know.

(g.k.)

in a final weep
she sat beneath my feet
i asked her why
and she said
for writing me

(g.k.)

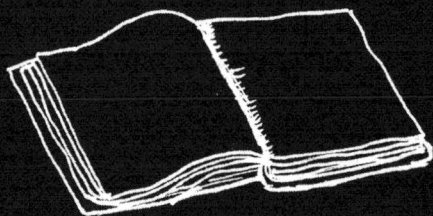

acknowledgments

i would like to first thank my audience. i would not be here without you. never will i be able to express how humble i am to receive all your support and love and kindness. i would also like to mention my closest friends for sticking with me through my hardships and victories. if it weren't for them and their constant encouragement, it would have been a much more bumpy ride. furthermore, i could not forget my beloved best friend, soul-mate, and the love of my life, Yana Prodanova. you have given me courage and warmth and you are one of the best things i could ever possibly be worthy of having. i love you very much.

       this book is meant to represent a bit of my heart in paper form. i'd like all to know how ecstatic i am that you've decided to let me share this fragile part of me

this is my days,

my dusks,

my darknesses,

and my dawns

and if you, my friend, have gotten this far, i know you'll live to see the rest of it.

Made in the USA
Las Vegas, NV
05 February 2022